Westward Expansion

AMERICA'S PUSH TO THE PACIFIC

SETTLERS, TRADERS, AND TRAILS

XINA M. UHL

Britannica
Educational Publishing

IN ASSOCIATION WITH

ROSEN
EDUCATIONAL SERVICES

Published in 2018 by Britannica Educational Publishing (a trademark of Encyclopædia Britannica, Inc.) in association with The Rosen Publishing Group, Inc.
29 East 21st Street, New York, NY 10010

Distributed exclusively by Rosen Publishing.
To see additional Britannica Educational Publishing titles, go to rosenpublishing.com.

First Edition

Britannica Educational Publishing
J.E. Luebering: Executive Director, Core Editorial
Andrea R. Field: Managing Editor, Compton's by Britannica

Rosen Publishing
Heather Moore Niver: Editor
Nelson Sá: Art Director
Tahara Anderson: Designer
Cindy Reiman: Photography Manager
Heather Moore Niver: Photo Researcher

Library of Congress Cataloging-in-Publication Data

Names: Uhl, Xina M., author.
Title: Settlers, traders, and trails / Xina M. Uhl.
Description: New York, NY : Britannica Educational Publishing, in Association with Rosen Educational Services, 2018 | Series: Westward expansion : America's push to the Pacific | Includes bibliographical references and index. | Audience: Grades 5–8.
Identifiers: LCCN 2017018668| ISBN 9781680487992 (library bound)
| ISBN 9781680487985 (pbk.) | ISBN 9781538300176 (6 pack)
Subjects: LCSH: United States—Territorial expansion—Juvenile literature. | West (U.S.)—History--Juvenile literature. | West (U.S.)—Discovery and exploration—Juvenile literature. | Frontier and pioneer life—West (U.S.)—Juvenile literature. | Pioneers—West (U.S.)—History—Juvenile literature.
Classification: LCC E179.5 .U35 2018 | DDC 978/.02—dc23
LC record available at https://lccn.loc.gov/2017018668

Manufactured in the United States of America

Photo credits: Cover, pp. 11, 15, 39 MPI/Archive Photos/Getty Images; pp. 5, 17, 28, 40 Bettmann/Getty Images; pp. 8, 10, 38 © North Wind Picture Archives; p. 12 Private Collection/Peter Newark American Pictures/Bridgeman Images; p. 19 Private Collection/©Look and Learn/Bridgeman Images; p. 20 Library of Congress, Washington, D.C.; p. 21 Peter Stackpole/The LIFE Picture Collection/Getty Images; p. 22 Print Collector/Hulton Archive/Getty Images; p. 24 Ed Vebell/Archive Photos/ Getty Images; p. 25 © National Park Service; p. 27 Time Life Pictures/The LIFE Picture Collection/Getty Images; p. 30 General Photographic Agency/Hulton Archive/Getty Images; p. 33 Courtesy of the Community of Christ, Independence, Missouri; pp. 34—35 Gladstone Collection/Library of Congress, Washington, D.C. (Digital File Number: cph 3g06161).

CONTENTS

INTRODUCTION

The settlement of the American colonies began in the early 1600s when English immigrants sailed across the Atlantic Ocean and settled at Jamestown and Plymouth Rock. The first years were full of peril and sickness, but the colonists endured and, over time, their colonies flourished. The boundaries of early America began expanding almost from the beginning of settlement. For the next three hundred years, settlers pushed the frontier westward, navigating first through dense forests and wide rivers, then across the endless plains and the towering mountains beyond, until at last they were stopped by the Pacific Ocean.

The original inhabitants of the lands, Native Americans, found their territory pushed farther westward. Weakened by diseases and overwhelmed by military conquest and the magnitude of white settlement, the American Indians gradually lost claim to their ancestral grounds.

Many settlers heading west traveled in groups of covered wagons. The wagons were filled with essential supplies, such as food, dishes, pots and pans, and clothing.

America's population kept increasing. Large numbers of people immigrated to the new country from Europe, and many of them moved to the West. The process of settling the whole of the continental United States would be marked by a host of difficulties that included rough terrain, harsh weather, and wars with Mexico and Native American tribes. The early settlers of the West faced countless challenges, yet their numbers continued to grow, and they fueled the relentless expansion across the country.

The hunger for land drove this westward push. Having land of one's own allowed settlers to make their own destinies, and hopefully forge a brighter future. The Louisiana Purchase in 1803 essentially doubled the size of the country. The annexation of Texas, a war with Mexico, negotiations with Britain—all added still more territory to the growing nation.

In the early 1800s, explorers, trappers, missionaries, and traders were the first white people to penetrate the lands beyond the Mississippi River. These bold adventurers sometimes forged agreements with Native Americans. At other times, they battled with them. The explorers created maps that lured gold miners, dirt farmers, cattle ranchers, and others to follow them. From Mormons looking for the Promised Land to wagon trains following thin, rough trails across the desolate frontier, settlers came by the thousands. Dangers they faced from injuries, exposure, illnesses, and attacks did not deter them. Their migration and homesteading marked the West as surely as did war and conflict. By the time the railroads spanned the continent, the days of the Wild West were numbered. Still, the romance of the frontier continued to define American culture, and persists even today.

CHAPTER ONE
EXPLORERS TRAVEL WEST

In 1492, Christopher Columbus crossed the Atlantic Ocean on behalf of Spain, hoping to find a new route to Asia. He failed in that quest, but he succeeded in finding a way to a New World that Europeans did not know existed.

The discovery of the New World—the Americas—seemed like a dream come true for many of the downtrodden in Europe. Famines, poverty, lack of work, oppressive governments, religious persecution, and the horrors of never-ending wars plagued many people. But the New World, with its open, unexplored lands, brimmed with promise. Before too long, large groups would risk death, disease, and disappointment for the chance at better lives.

THE FIRST INHABITANTS

The Americas had been settled long before the arrival of Europeans by many millions of people. These original

Among the earliest European settlers in the New World were the Puritans. Having endured religious persecution in England, they came to America to establish a new religious denomination.

occupants are now known collectively as American Indians or Native Americans. At the time of European contact, American Indians inhabited most of what would become the United States. In the Northeast, these tribes included the Massachuset, Pequot, and Iroquois. In the Southeast, they included the Cherokee, Seminole, and Choctaw. Across the Great Plains roamed the Sioux, Cheyenne, and Pawnee. The Southwest cultures included the Navajo, Pueblo, and Apache. In the West lived the Shoshone, Chumash, and Ute. In the Northwest dwelled the Chinook, Yakima, and Nez Percé.

When Europeans came, they brought diseases like smallpox, typhoid, and cholera. The Native Americans, having been isolated from the Old World, had no immunity to these diseases, and they died in devastating epidemics. DNA evidence suggests that about half of those alive following contact with Europeans died of disease, war, or enslavement.

THE EUROPEANS COME

In the sixteenth century, Spain conquered and colonized large areas in the New World, including what are now Florida, California, and the Southwestern United States. In the seventeenth century, England established settlements along the Atlantic coast that later became the thirteen original American colonies. By the eighteenth century, France held the valleys of the St. Lawrence, Ohio, Alabama, and Mississippi rivers, as well as large tracts of land to the west, and Holland claimed large parts of what became New York State. Each of these countries came to America looking to use the land's resources and establish trade.

The Spanish established missions in California that raised sheep and cattle for trade. The French hunted for furs and exported them, and the English farmed crops like tobacco and cotton. In 1803, President Thomas Jefferson negotiated the purchase of France's

Spanish missionaries were among the first to introduce Native Americans to Christianity. The goal of the missions was to incorporate Indian tribes into Spanish culture.

holdings west of the Mississippi River in what became known as the Louisiana Purchase. This land included most of fifteen present-day states. Jefferson sent Meriwether Lewis and William Clark in 1804 on a great expedition to explore this uncharted land. They found hundreds of plant and animal species previously unknown to science, dozens of American Indian tribes, and the Rocky Mountains. The routes they took and maps they penned greatly influenced later travelers.

This painting shows Lewis and Clark's Shoshone Indian interpreter, Sacajawea, communicating with the local Native American inhabitants.

THE INDIAN REMOVAL ACT

Businessmen and settlers alike wanted to make use of lands to the west. Unfortunately, their ambitions would come at a severe cost to Native Americans. In

1763, before the United States proclaimed its independence, the British government had designated the land between the Appalachian Mountains and the Mississippi River for use by Native Americans.

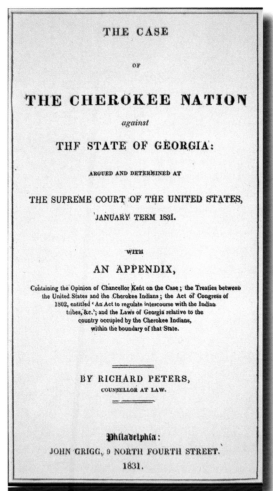

THE CASE

OF

THE CHEROKEE NATION

against

THE STATE OF GEORGIA:

ARGUED AND DETERMINED AT

THE SUPREME COURT OF THE UNITED STATES,

JANUARY TERM 1831.

WITH

AN APPENDIX,

Containing the Opinion of Chancellor Kent on the Case; the Treaties between the United States and the Cherokee Indians; the Act of Congress of 1802, entitled 'An Act to regulate intercourse with the Indian tribes, &c.'; and the Laws of Georgia relative to the country occupied by the Cherokee Indians, within the boundary of that State.

BY RICHARD PETERS,
COUNSELLOR AT LAW.

Philadelphia:
JOHN GRIGG, 9 NORTH FOURTH STREET.
1831.

Even though the Cherokee Nation won the Supreme Court case to allow them to stay on their lands, they were still forced to move.

American settlers trespassed on this land, however, and by 1829, when gold was discovered on Cherokee land in Georgia, many whites scarcely recognized Native Americans claims to the land. In 1830, the US Congress passed the Indian Removal Act, authorizing the forced relocation of the Indians to territory west of the Mississippi River.

Some tribes quickly negotiated the turnover of their lands and moved west. The Seminole fiercely resisted before their eventual defeat

MORE ABOUT THE TRAIL OF TEARS

Many of the Native Americans forced to migrate because of the 1830 Indian Removal Act were Cherokee. They had traded and intermarried with white settlers, and over time, took on many American customs. Despite this, more than 90 percent of their homelands were transferred to whites between 1721 and 1819. In 1832 the Cherokee successfully sued the state of Georgia in the Supreme Court. The court ruled that the states did not have the right to impose regulations on Indian land. However, Georgia did not follow the court's decision, and President Andrew Jackson refused to enforce it. Instead, he advocated for Indian removal.

In 1838 the US military began to force the Cherokee from their homes, often at gunpoint. Held in miserable camps for days or weeks before their journeys began, many became ill; overcrowding and poor sanitation resulted in many deaths.

The forced march took place over 116 days in the winter of 1838. The trail stretched more than eight hundred miles (about twelve hundred kilometers). Most of the Indians were poorly equipped for the grueling journey. They traveled through heavy rains, ice storms, and poor roads through a land with little game or other food. The trip was especially brutal for small children and the elderly. Of the roughly fifteen thousand Cherokee who made the journey, some four thousand perished.

and removal. The Cherokee, after attempting a legal challenge, were forcibly removed and set on the long journey west.

Overall, the US government forced roughly one hundred thousand American Indians to leave their homes and move west. Most of the Indians made the journey on foot. About fifteen thousand died during the trip, which is remembered as the Trail of Tears.

MANIFEST DESTINY

After Lewis and Clark's famous expedition, politicians, journalists, settlers, and others came to embrace the idea that it was America's destiny from God to take over the land from the East to West coasts and to establish democracy and Christianity there. This perspective was captured in a newspaper editorial in 1845 by the journalist John O'Sullivan, who described it as "manifest destiny." The term stuck and a new worldview was born.

Traders led the way west of the Mississippi River, cutting trails through prairies and across the rugged Rocky Mountains. The Santa Fe Trail was one of the most important trade routes. Though Native Americans had used sections of the trail for centuries, Captain William Becknell officially blazed the entire route in 1821. It extended from Independence, Missouri, to

This 1839 engraving shows a wagon train forming a defensive circle at a traders' camp on the Santa Fe Trail.

what is now Santa Fe, New Mexico, a journey that took from six to eight weeks through raging rivers and parched deserts. Despite untold hardships, the unrelenting westward movement would ultimately cover what is now the United States, stretching "from sea to shining sea."

CHAPTER TWO

FUR FEVER

When it came to opening the West to white settlement, traders and trappers made as great a contribution as that of Lewis and Clark. The fur trappers, called mountain men, roamed the West from about 1806, when Lewis and Clark returned from their expedition, to around 1840, when the westward migration of settlers came to dominate the trails. Trappers could make good money selling furs, which they found in abundance in the American frontier. The popularity in Europe of men's beaver hats was a key factor driving the trade.

Mountain men freely roamed the Rocky Mountains and the Sierra Nevada range. They followed rivers and streams full of otter and beaver and brought back tales of huge redwood trees, gushing geysers, and green, lush valleys. With their full beards and fringed buckskin clothing, the men seemed half-wild themselves.

This drawing shows traders and trappers meeting at the annual rendezvous near Scotts Bluff, Nebraska.

On the trail they spent months away from other people, which only added to their mystique. The realities of life on the trail were somewhat less romantic, however. The men suffered from bitter cold, scorching heat waves, and attacks from both Native Americans and wild animals such as grizzly bears.

Once or twice a year in summer, the mountain men gathered at a rendezvous where they traded furs for supplies, swapped stories, and held boisterous gatherings. In his memoirs, Jim Beckwourth, an African American mountain man, described the gatherings as rowdy parties filled with singing, dancing, shouting, and drinking, as well as racing and target shooting.

Because of the danger and isolation, one in five mountain men died on the trail. By 1840, beaver hats were out of style and the demand for beaver furs diminished. In addition, trappers had depleted the supply of beavers almost entirely. Some mountain men became guides for the army or for wagon trains that carried settlers to Oregon and California.

JOHN COLTER: MOUNTAIN MAN

One of the first mountain men was John Colter, who had been a member of the Lewis and Clark Expedition. He was an excellent hunter and guide, and the group relied on him to help navigate rivers and find passes through mountains. Around 1806, Colter left the expedition to join up with two trappers who were working along the upper Missouri River. The following year he joined an expedition led by Manuel Lisa, another famous trapper. They built a fort and trading post named Fort Raymond on the Yellowstone River in south-central Montana.

Lisa later sent Colter on a mission to scout areas west and south and to invite Native American tribes to trade at the fort. Colter headed off in the dead of winter to travel alone through parts of Montana, Idaho, and Wyoming, covering hundreds of miles. He is thought to have been the first white man to see the Grand Teton mountain range, Jackson Hole, and the Yellowstone valley, with its hot springs, geysers, and other wonders.

In three expeditions to the Three Forks area in Montana in 1808–10, Colter narrowly escaped with his life in battles involving warring Indian tribes. He later retired to a farm on the Missouri River.

John Colter is shown here in the characteristic costume of the mountain men—buckskin decorated with fringes.

MERCHANTS AND MISSIONARIES

In the early days of fur trading, enterprising business-men like John Jacob Astor realized that they could find many valuable furs in the Oregon Territory. Astor established the Pacific Fur Company in 1810 at Fort Astoria, Oregon. In need of supplies, the company sent explorer Robert Stuart, a member of Astor's company, back east in 1812. Stuart and his party discovered a 20-mile (32-km) gap in the Rocky Mountains in south-western Wyoming. The South Pass, as it came to be known, offered the lowest and easiest crossing of the Continental Divide, a north-south ridge through the Rockies. The South Pass did not become well known

A bustling center for the fur trade, Fort Astoria was operated by Pacific Fur Company employees, a diverse group that included Scots, Native Americans, French Canadians, Americans, and Native Hawaiians.

until 1824, after which it was used extensively, becoming a key passage on routes to the Far West.

Missionaries traveled into the Oregon Territory early on. Marcus and Narcissa Whitman were among the earliest and most significant. In 1836, they headed west with another missionary couple, Henry Harmon Spalding and his wife, Eliza. Narcissa and Eliza were the first white women known to cross the Continental Divide. The Whitmans established a mission among the Cayuse Indians near today's Walla Walla, Washington, while the Spaldings set up a mission among the Nez Percé Indians in southern Idaho.

In 1842, Marcus Whitman journeyed 3,000 miles (4,828 km) back east to ask his sponsors for support to continue the mission. He also met with government officials, informing them of Oregon's merits for settlers. On his return journey, he joined a caravan of almost 1,000 settlers that later became known as the "great migration."

Marcus Whitman and his wife Narcissa (*pictured above*) were among the first missionaries to travel to the Oregon Territory.

A military officer, explorer, and mapmaker, John C. Frémont was a key figure in opening up the American West and played a key role in the US conquest and development of California.

In 1847, the Whitmans realized that the Cayuse Indians they served were becoming increasingly hostile. When a measles epidemic broke out, the Indians suspected the family of practicing sorcery. On November 29 of that year, the Indians attacked, killing fourteen whites, including the Whitmans, and kidnapping fifty-three women and children.

A key figure in opening up the American West was the explorer and mapmaker John C. Frémont. Between 1842 and 1847 he led three major expeditions to the Far West, mapping much of the territory between the Mississippi valley and the Pacific Ocean. Frémont's work, coupled with the efforts of missionaries and reports of fertile land, set the stage for the massive westward movement of settlers in the 1840s that came to be known as "Oregon Fever."

CHAPTER THREE
WESTWARD HO!

In 1818, the United States acquired the Red River Basin through an agreement with Great Britain, and in 1819, the Onís-Adams Treaty with Spain brought Florida into the country. In 1821, Mexico won independence from Spain and took control of Spain's western lands in North America. In 1846, the United States and Mexico went to war over a dispute regarding the boundary of Texas. US President James K. Polk had pushed the country toward war with his policy on Texas and his desire to bring California into the country. Though the Mexican-American War was unpopular in general, those who favored expansion supported it. In 1848, the United States won the war, and the subsequent agreement, known as the Mexican Cession, brought into the country all or parts of present-day California, Nevada, Utah, Wyoming, Colorado, Arizona, and New Mexico.

A dispute with the British over the boundary of Oregon also was settled under President Polk. In 1846, he negotiated a treaty that gave the United States the lands south of the 49th parallel (latitude 49°N). This land was later carved into the states of Washington and Oregon and part of Idaho.

In 1853, the United States paid Mexico $10 million for the Gadsden Purchase, a narrow strip of land in southern Arizona and New Mexico. With this purchase the continental United States came to exist in its present form, from "sea to shining sea." Two other

James Gadsen, the president of the South Carolina Railroad Company, negotiated with Mexico to purchase the land later known as the Gadsen Purchase. Gadsen hoped to build a railroad there.

territories were acquired later: Alaska (purchased from Russia in 1867) and Hawaii (annexed in 1898).

THE OREGON TRAIL

The two most important trails west were the Santa Fe Trail and the Oregon Trail. Both started in Independence, Missouri. The Santa Fe Trail stretched southwest about 900 miles (1,450 km) across the Western plains to Santa Fe, New Mexico. Traders used the trail to send manufactured goods to Santa Fe and silver and furs back to the East. Although settlers also used the Santa Fe Trail to

Chimney Rock was one of the most famous landmarks for pioneers traveling westward. It is located on the south edge of the North Platte River Valley near present-day Bayard, Nebraska.

move to New Mexico, Colorado, and other parts of the West, the trail was primarily a commercial route.

The Oregon Trail was the chief westward route for hundreds of thousands of settlers from the 1840s through the 1860s. It angled northwest from Independence, spanning about 2,000 miles (3,200 km). It consisted of paths that had already been discovered by explorers, fur traders, and missionaries. Wagon trains set off in the spring and traveled for four to six months, passing through the deep-rooted grasses of the Great Plains. They had to get through the Rocky Mountains before winter hit and freezing temperatures endangered their lives.

THE PRAIRIE SCHOONERS

The most popular covered wagon on the great westward trails was known as the prairie schooner. It was a small, light wagon covered by a white canvas bonnet and pulled along by teams of ten to twelve horses or mules, or six pairs of oxen yoked together. Travelers preferred mules or oxen because they were hardier than horses for long-distance travel.

The covered wagons were designed to carry cargo, not passengers. They had little room, so tools and supplies got most of the space. These included things like water buckets, grease buckets, ropes, hammers, buckskin for repairing saddles and bridles, trunks packed with dishes, butter churns, coffee grinders, and food supplies like flour and sugar. Often people tried to carry extra items like dressers and other furniture. Much of the time these extras were unloaded and left in the prairie to lighten the wagons.

Wagon wheels were made of wood with metal bands. The wagons had no suspensions, which meant that the rides were so rough that people often preferred to walk rather than ride and be jolted back and forth.

Tools, clothing, blankets, buckets, and cooking supplies were the most important cargo items in the prairie schooners. There was little room for passengers, so travelers often walked alongside the wagons.

Unlike the harsh conditions of the dry and dusty Santa Fe route, the Oregon Trail had access to water, easy river and stream crossings, pasture for horses and livestock, and low passes through the mountains. The trip was anything but easy, however. Pioneers set out by the thousands, mainly in covered wagons pulled by teams of draft animals. They covered an average of 15 to 20 miles (24 to 32 km) per day at a rate of only 1 to 2 miles (1.6 to 3.2 km) per hour, or about 100 miles (161 km) a week. Traveling with other settlers in wagon trains brought some protection. In the evenings, they drew their wagons into a circle to keep the cattle from wandering off. The travelers faced Indian attacks, raging river crossings, choking dust, lack of shade, hot temperatures, disease, and injury. One out of every ten pioneers who traveled the trail died on it.

An estimated 300,000 to 400,000 people used the Oregon Trail during its heyday from the mid-1840s to the late 1860s. Many emigrants traveled into Oregon, where

This illustration shows how pioneers on a wagon train bound for Oregon might have spent their evening hours.

they established a claim to the land. A large number, however, left the trail near what is now Idaho to follow a southwestward branch called the California Trail.

THE CALIFORNIA GOLD RUSH

Once the Mexican-American War ended, Americans from the East began making their way into the new state of California. In January 1848, James Marshall found a gold nugget in a ditch as he worked on a sawmill on John Sutter's land near the Sacramento River. Gold had been discovered! The news spread like wildfire across the country and internationally. By the next year, eager gold miners streamed into California, expecting to get rich. The California Gold Rush had begun.

Around eighty thousand "forty-niners" (as the fortune seekers of 1849 were called) descended on California. They quickly overran the area around Sutter's mill, then spread out to scour the Sacramento Valley. They dug into the land with picks and shovels, and panned for gold in streams. Within four years the number of fortune seekers grew to about 250,000. Mining towns developed overnight. Law and order was scarce, so vigilantes punished crimes. Whatever gold lay above ground was snatched up quickly, so miners dug underground to locate lodes.

One method used by prospectors to find gold was to pour water in a pan and add dirt. The prospectors then swirled the water gently, looking for shiny pieces of gold.

Most of the forty-niners found no gold at all; however, the merchants who sold supplies and services like laundering profited by charging high prices to the desperate miners. The influx of people during the gold rush helped to establish many of today's towns in California.

KLONDIKE GOLD

California wasn't the only source of gold in North America. Other small gold rushes occurred at various points throughout the nineteenth century, including discoveries in Georgia, Nevada, Colorado, and South Dakota. In 1896, prospectors found gold along the Klondike River, in Canada's Yukon territory. News of the discovery produced an uproar across America. People quit their jobs and hurried north. About one hundred thousand prospectors set out for the Yukon, but only about thirty thousand made it to their destination. Rugged mountains, frozen rivers, blizzards, and lack of food confronted the prospectors. Many gave up; others died along the way. The miners who reached the Klondike found the mining hard work. Permafrost made digging for gold difficult. Boom towns sprang up near mining claims along rivers. The Klondike rush produced millions of dollars in gold over several years. Production soon dropped, however, and by 1910 most of the population had left the region.

CHAPTER FOUR

NO PLACE LIKE HOME

The common experience the pioneers shared helped to forge a national identity. People in the West did not regard themselves as citizens of a particular territory or state, but as citizens of the United States. However, a strong independence still marked the pioneer experience of many groups.

MORMONS COME WEST

The open lands of the West beckoned to many who sought freedom from persecution. Among those seeking such peace were the Mormons, followers of the Church of Jesus Christ of Latter-day Saints.

The church was established in 1830 by Joseph Smith, a New York farmer who published the Book of Mormon, which he said was a divinely inspired holy book. He quickly gathered followers, but some of the church's beliefs brought trouble with local governments. The church moved several times because hostile communities drove them out. In Illinois, Smith was murdered by an angry mob.

In 1844, Brigham Young took control of the church. Hoping to find the church a permanent home, he led a group of Mormon settlers on the long and dangerous journey west. They split off from the Oregon Trail

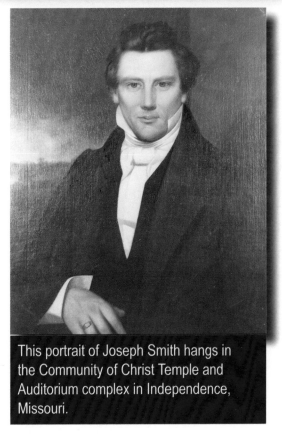

This portrait of Joseph Smith hangs in the Community of Christ Temple and Auditorium complex in Independence, Missouri.

at the Platte River, taking the north bank along what would become known as the Mormon Trail. In July 1847, Young and 148 emigrants arrived at the Great Salt Lake. To build the population, Young encouraged missionaries to convert others to the faith. By 1869, about eighty thousand Mormon pioneers were settled in more than three hundred communities in Utah and neighboring territories.

The church came into conflict with the US government on many issues. One of the most significant was the Mormon practice of polygamy, or multiple marriage, which was illegal in the rest of the United States. The church officially discontinued the practice in 1890, and in 1896 Utah entered the Union as a state.

AFRICAN AMERICAN SETTLERS

Prior to the Thirteenth Amendment to the Constitution, which freed all slaves, slavery was prohibited in "free states" such as California and most northern states but was permitted in the South. The western territories of Utah and New Mexico (and later Kansas and Nebraska) could decide for themselves whether or not they wanted to allow slavery there. This meant

American Indians gave black soldiers the nickname "Buffalo Soldiers," though the significance of the name is unclear.

A WOMAN HOMESTEADER

In 1909, Elinore Pruitt Stewart was living in Denver with her small daughter Jerrine. Discouraged by a life of poverty, she answered a newspaper ad for a housekeeper for Clyde Stewart in Burntfork, Wyoming. She and Jerrine traveled to Wyoming and claimed a homestead next to Clyde's property. Eight weeks later, she and Clyde married. This excerpt from one of her letters provides a glimpse into the life of a woman homesteader.

When I read of the hard times among the Denver poor, I feel like urging them every one to get out and file on land. I am very enthusiastic about women homesteading . . . Even if improving the place does go slowly, it is that much done to stay done. Whatever is raised is the homesteader's own, and there is no house-rent to pay. This year Jerrine cut and dropped enough potatoes to raise a ton of fine potatoes. She wanted to try, so we let her, and you will remember that she is but six years old. We had a man to break the ground and cover the potatoes for her and the man irrigated them once. That was all that was done until digging time, when they were ploughed out and Jerrine picked them up. Any woman strong enough to go out by the day could have done every bit of the work and put in two or three times that much, and it would have been so much more pleasant than to work so hard in the city and then be on starvation rations in the winter.

To me, homesteading is the solution of all poverty's problems, but I realize that temperament has much to do with success in any undertaking, and persons afraid of coyotes and work and loneliness had better let ranching alone.

that African Americans could be free in certain areas in the United States. After slavery became illegal, some freed slaves joined the flood of settlers headed west. Though they faced discrimination, African Americans were found in all walks of life. They were ranchers, cowboys, farmers, trappers, explorers, gold miners, Army scouts, lawmen, schoolteachers, saloonkeepers, and more. All-black army units called Buffalo Soldiers clashed with Native Americans on the Great Plains.

While no one is sure just how many African Americans came west, a few are known because they became famous. Nat Love became a champion roper and cowboy who herded cattle, survived stampedes and gunfights, and weathered the heat and cold of the open prairie. Bass Reeves won fourteen shootouts with outlaws as a deputy US marshal in Oklahoma. Mary Fields, known as Stagecoach Mary, went to Montana

Native Americans fought the United States in the Plains Wars (1850s–1870s), a series of battles over control of the Great Plains. Among the worst of the battles was the Sand Creek Massacre, in which 150 Cheyenne were killed.

in 1884 at the age of fifty-two. A powerful woman, the gun-toting Mary stood six feet (eight meters) tall and smoked homemade cigars. She did many jobs, including running a restaurant and a laundry, and working for the local nuns in the fields, but she became best known for driving a stagecoach to deliver the US mail.

MAKING HOMES AND TAKING THEM AWAY

As more white settlers established farms, ranches, towns, and roads through the West, they came into conflict with

This family in Loup Valley, Nebraska, is heading to their new home-stead as a result of the Homestead Act of 1862.

Native Americans. Control of the Great Plains was especially contentious, leading to numerous battles between the US government and the Plains Indians. In 1864, approximately seven hundred US soldiers attacked a Cheyenne camp. Although the Cheyenne had already surrendered, the soldiers slaughtered more than 150 of them in what is known as the Sand Creek Massacre.

However, the Plains Indians didn't always lose such battles. In Montana in 1876, General George Armstrong

Custer took a few hundred men to drive back forces assembled by the Sioux chiefs Crazy Horse and Sitting Bull. Custer did not realize that the Sioux outnumbered them by about four thousand. What followed would later be called Custer's Last Stand as he and his men—except for one Indian scout—were killed.

Despite skirmishes with tribes throughout the West, the United States established peace with Native Americans by the early twentieth century.

The family shown here in Custer County, Nebraska, was one of the hundreds of thousands of families that received land through the Homestead Act.

The Homestead Act of 1862 was meant to hasten the settlement of the West. It stated that anyone older than twenty-one years of age who had never taken up arms against the US government—including women and freed slaves—could claim 160 acres (65 hectares) of federal land. They had to build a house on the land and farm it, but after living there for five years they became the owners. Most of the people who took advantage of the act were families, though single women and widows, some with children, also claimed homesteads.

A HARD ROW TO HOE

Western pioneers had difficult, lonely lives for the most part. Many were poor. They used hand tools to clear the land, build shelters, and plant crops. Disease, storms, floods, and injuries occurred frequently. Law and order was slow to arrive in many towns, and outlaws stole and killed in frightening attacks. Cowboys tended herds of cattle on horseback, driving them to market in far-off towns like Abilene, Kansas, and Chicago in long cattle drives.

Railroads made the trip to the West easier and quicker. After the Civil War ended, an increasing number of lines appeared across the frontier. Still, pioneers continued to use the wagon trails until about 1880.

By 1870 only portions of the Great Plains could truly be called unsettled. For most of the next two decades, that land functioned as the fabled open range, home to cowboys and their grazing cattle. But by the late 1880s, the range cattle industry was declining. Settlers moved in and fenced the Great Plains into family farms. That settlement essentially constituted the last chapter of the westward movement. By the early 1890s, for the first time in American history, the frontier had ceased to exist.

GLOSSARY

annex To add a territory to another to make a bigger country.

buckskin Leather that is soft and flexible.

continental Occurring on or spanning a continent.

Continental Divide The highest point of land in North America that separates the waters that flow west from those flowing north or east; most of the Divide runs along the crest of Rocky Mountains.

covered wagon A wooden wagon with a top formed into an arch and covered with canvas.

export To send something out of a country to sell in another country.

exposure The condition of being unprotected from the elements, especially the cold.

forty-niners People who came to California beginning in 1849 to collect or mine gold.

Great Plains A broad, flat area west of the Mississippi River and east of the Rocky Mountains that is covered in grasslands.

homestead A piece of land acquired from the government by filing a claim and then living on and farming the land.

latitude A distance north or south of the equator that is measured in degrees.

lode A deposit of ore.

Manifest Destiny A belief in nineteenth-century America that the expansion of the country across the continent was willed by God.

measles A contagious illness caused by a virus that produces a fever and red spots on the skin.

mountain men Trappers and explorers who lived in the wilderness of the western mountain ranges in the United States.

permafrost A layer of permanently frozen earth under the surface.

pioneer One of the first people to settle in a new area.

polygamy The practice of having more than one wife at the same time.

prairie A large area of rolling land characterized by deep, fertile soil, tall grasses, and few trees.

prospector A person who seeks riches, usually through the mining of ore.

rendezvous A meeting planned in advance.

vigilante A person or group of people who punish criminals outside of the law.

wagon train A column of wagons traveling overland; in US history, the wagons that carried pioneers westward.

yoke A wooden bar that joins two draft animals together by the neck in order to pull a load.

FOR FURTHER READING

Dolan, Edward F. *Beyond the Frontier: The Story of the Trails West (Great Journeys)*. New York, NY: Benchmark Books, 2000.

Hale, Nathan. *Donner Dinner Party.* New York, NY: Harry N. Abrams, 2013.

Holub, Joan. *What Was the Gold Rush?* New York, NY: Grosset & Dunlap, 2013.

Honders, Christine. *Buffalo Soldiers.* Milwaukee, WI: Gareth Stevens Publishing, 2015.

Schanzer, Rosalyn. *How We Crossed The West: The Adventures Of Lewis And Clark*. Washington, DC: National Geographic Children's Books, 2002.

Schlissel, Lillian. *Black Frontiers: A History of African American Heroes in the Old West.* New York, NY: Simon & Schuster, 2000.

Sheinkin, Steve. *Which Way to the Wild West? Everything Your Schoolbooks Didn't Tell You About Westward Expansion*. New York, NY: Square Fish, 2015.

Stanley, George Edward. *Davy Crockett: Frontier Legend.* New York, NY. Sterling Publishing, 2008.

WEBSITES

Because of the changing nature of internet links, Rosen Publishing has developed an online list of websites related to the subject of this book. This site is updated regularly. Please use this link to access this list:

http://www.rosenlinks.com/WEST/Trails

INDEX